ACTION SPORTS

SNOCROSS

KENNY ABDO

abdopublishing.com

Published by Abdo Zoom, a division of ABDO, P.O. Box 398166, Minneapolis, Minnesota 55439. Copyright © 2018 by Abdo Consulting Group, Inc. International copyrights reserved in all countries. No part of this book may be reproduced in any form without written permission from the publisher.

Printed in the United States of America, North Mankato, Minnesota.
092017
012018

THIS BOOK CONTAINS
RECYCLED MATERIALS

Photo Credits: Alamy, Icon Sportswire, iStock, Shutterstock
Production Contributors: Kenny Abdo, Jennie Forsberg, Grace Hansen
Design Contributors: Dorothy Toth, Neil Klinepier

Publisher's Cataloging-in-Publication Data

Names: Abdo, Kenny, author.
Title: Snocross / by Kenny Abdo.
Description: Minneapolis, Minnesota: Abdo Zoom, 2018. | Series: Action sports |
    Includes online resource and index.
Identifiers: LCCN 2017939267 | ISBN 9781532120954 (lib.bdg.) |
    ISBN 9781532122071 (ebook) | ISBN 9781532122637 (Read-to-Me ebook)
Subjects: LCSH: Snocross--Juvenile literature. | Winter Sports--Juvenile literature
    Extreme Sports— Juvenile literature.
Classification: DDC 796.9--dc23
LC record available at https://lccn.loc.gov/2017939267

TABLE OF CONTENTS

SNOCROSS

Snocross is an extreme sport held on the snow. High performance snowmobiles **race** on **man-made** or natural **trails**.

The sport is similar to motocross. But it uses a snowmobile instead of a dirt bike, and snow instead of dirt.

TYPES

There are four major snowmobile manufactures. They are Arctic Cat, BRP, Polaris, and Yamaha.

Snocross snowmobiles have small **engines**, but are extremely fast.

Higher-powered snowmobiles can reach speeds of 150 miles per hour (241 kph). **Drag racing** snowmobiles can go higher than 200 miles per hour (322 kph).

Most jumps are more than 30 feet (9.1 m) tall. Riders travel up to 130 feet (39.6 m) before they touch the ground.

RACES

Snocross is popular in the United States, Canada, and some parts of Europe. All **races** are held during the **winter** months.

Snocross competitions happen across the world every year. It has been a major event during the Winter **X Games** since 1998.

Petter Narsa from Sweden won the gold medal in the Snowmobile SnoCross event at **X Games** Aspen 2017.

GLOSSARY

drag racing – a race between two vehicles for a short distance.

engine – a machine that changes power into motion.

man-made – made by humans.

race – a competition of speed.

trails – a path created to travel through rough terrain.

X Games – an extreme sports event held every year by ESPN.

ONLINE RESOURCES

Booklinks
NONFICTION NETWORK
FREE! ONLINE NONFICTION RESOURCES

To learn more about snocross, please visit **abdobooklinks.com**. These links are routinely monitored and updated to provide the most current information available.

INDEX